WHAT THE HELL IS LIFE???

HELPING YOU TO UNDERSTAND LIFE AND HOW TO GET THE MOST OUT OF IT

AISHA GORDON-HILES

Instagram: @selfforhelp

E-mail: selfforhelp@gmail.com

Future publications: Social media sucks (coming soon)

Contents

About the author:

Hi! I am Aisha Gordon-Hiles. I am a qualified integrative Counsellor, from the UK. I have worked for many years in a counselling capacity with individuals of all ages, races, genders and cultures.

As well as being a Counsellor I also run a self-help Instagram page called @selfforhelp. Through this page and writing this book I am starting a journey of being able to help the world.

My whole life I have had an interest in writing but, I had not taken it seriously until now. This book is the first in my series of self-help material to enhance the accessibility of professional help for all.

Preface: What is this book for?

Through many conversations and my own experiences, I have come to realise a common theme in struggles and that is around life... I have heard questions such as "am I doing it right?" as well as statements advising people to "live their best life" and judgments such as "he/she is wasting their life away". All of these suggest that there is some right or ideal way to "do" life and so I began to wonder... "If that is the case, then where do you find out about this?"

The aim of this book is to aid your reflections on life and offer one way in which you can understand and manage it to bring about happiness and change. I will share with you my metaphor for life and how it has helped me understand and get the best out of it. We will explore the self and the limitations we put on ourselves in life. And in doing so, help you to decide what you want your life to be like and find out how you will get there.

There are a series of activities in this book designed to help you reflect on you and your life. Some of the activities may feel hard to do as our bodies and minds can struggle with change and self-reflection. If you find yourself struggling, ask a friend to help you. They will be more objective in activities that require you to be honest about yourself. All activities can be completed in this book or on a separate piece of paper.

💡 (when you see this symbol in the book it means I have a tip for you)

Disclaimer

This information and advice is given to you to help aid your reflection and understanding of life. It does not claim to be the only solution or way of getting the best out of life. I am aware I will not know all the individual circumstances of all the people who choose to read this book. Thus, I cannot accept any liability for the consequences of reading the material in the book. If you feel uncomfortable issues and feelings arise for you as a consequence of reading this book please seek assistance from a qualified mental health professional or your doctor.

Author's process notes

As I explained in the preface, everything in this book has been tried and tested by me. As a rule of thumb, I do not recommend anything that I have not tried myself to anyone. I think it is important to really know how it feels to undertake anything I recommend. I feel it is important to have insight on how an activity might feel for the person I am recommending it to. With that being said, I wanted to share a little about my own process of going through the sections in this book to help me achieve my goal of writing it.

After I had decided to write this book I noticed I immediately started telling people about it... why? Well, firstly because I was excited. Secondly, because I knew I would find a way to talk myself out of it or not go through with it if I started to feel anxious. So, by telling people about it, I made myself accountable!

The second thing I noticed was, the process of telling people about it was almost like "market research". Seeing people's responses enabled me to see if it was worth doing or not. The more I told people and the more interested responses I got, the more I was inspired to write.

About halfway through writing this book I noticed anxiety had kicked in. I had told people about it which meant they were expecting to see it and read it. I noticed in my writing I had used the words book and booklet interchangeably and while proofreading I asked myself why.

I began to realise, I was calling this book a booklet to lower people's expectations of it, so that if people didn't like it, it wouldn't hurt me so much. But I realised in doing that I was saying my book was going to be a "failure". So, I sat myself down and with the help of others I acknowledged what I was doing. I reassured myself that I was doing what I wanted and it was the right thing to do.

I wanted to include these notes because I think it is important to acknowledge my own "humanness" in this process. I may be a therapist, but I still get anxious too and have struggled with self-doubt and fear along the way.

Dedication and acknowledgements

This book marks my learning about life and is a step towards creating the life I want to live. There have been many challenges along the way with the biggest one being my own fears. I couldn't have done it without my mother, grandmother and father being role models of hard work and the two former being excellent writers themselves so to all of you – Thank you!

I couldn't have done it without my best friends Chioma, Giovanna, Jade and Jennifer who have been great examples to be led by and have helped me finalise this book. To all of you – Thank you!

I also could not have done it without Jamal Ajose-George who has pushed and encouraged me to face my fears and become the best possible version of me. – Thank you!

Finally, I would like to say a massive thank you to Yousuf Ullah for helping me transform my images, to my wonderful clients over the years and my followers on Instagram for giving me the confidence in my words.

"Ultimately, we are all experts of ourselves, sometimes we just need help to see it"
- Self For Help

One

"As we get older, we have an important choice to make: To BE or not to BE-come our parents" - Self For Help

Firrst off, let me start by saying, this section is not intended to rupture the relationships you have with your parents by any means! What I mean when I say we have the choice to be or not be our parents is:

"We need to take a look at ourselves and our behaviours and learn from the behaviours of those who brought us up. This helps us to become the person that WE want to be".

But before we get into that, let's start at the beginning.

***

When we are born, we are pretty much a blank canvas. We have our 5 senses (which will continue to refine and develop themselves), the implicit (unconscious) memories of our time in the womb and two fears. The fear of falling and the fear of loud noises.

In short, everything that you know today is a consequence of the experiences you have had in your life and the people in it. For most, the first people to shape our sense of identity are our parents. However, this is not the case for all and in that case, it would be whoever your primary caregivers were.

As babies we look to the people we spend the most time around to show us how to survive life. It is from these people that we develop our likes, loves, fears and wants. If you take a second to reflect on your primary caregivers you will see that bits of their personalities and mannerisms are similar if not exactly the same as yours.

Has anyone ever said to you "you sound so much like your..." or "you are so much like your..."? This will be because you have picked aspects of them to help you manage and understand the world around you as you were growing up. This process is called mirroring.

Now interestingly enough, this passing down of traits and habits does not have to be through actual contact. This is seen when people display characteristics of people in their families that they have never met or have spent little time with. This is caused by the passing down of genetics. Either way, whether it be through genetics or mirroring, our sense of self and personality is influenced.

Now, the whole point of this book is to help you learn how to get the best out of the life you have. To help you be the version of you that you want to be. And I'm assuming you are reading this book because there is something you want to change or understand. So, I guess I should get on with getting you there... Let's start by understanding exactly who you are...

The task I am about to ask you to do is something you can do over and over in your life as new things pop up.

It is something you can complete here in this book or on a separate piece of paper. The goal is that, with time, the more you do it the more it will become part of your natural way of being.

💡 Tip: "It does get easier to do" if you find you are struggling, especially the first time around… Ask someone who knows you and your family well, to help you.

First, identify the people you spent the most time with between the ages of 0 and 4 to 5 years old.

Now the next parts can be done in any order, whichever feels most comfortable.

💡 Tip, if you really want to understand yourself more, pay attention to which part you gravitate towards answering first in the next parts and ask yourself why.

Next, make a list of all your traits, habits and parts of your personality that you are aware of. These can be both positive and negative. They can be things you like about yourself, things you want to change about yourself or both (I have put in a few examples to get you started).

(Eg: Caring, spiteful, hardworking, angry).

Now, make a list of the most memorable traits, habits and personality parts of the people who you listed in the first section. Again, these can be positive or negative.

(What are your memories of those people? How did they behave towards others? How did they behave towards you?)

Okay great, you made it through that! You might think I'm being sarcastic but it's not the easiest thing to do because it requires you to be honest with yourself. This is something a lot of people struggle with. If you feel like you weren't entirely honest with yourself then please go back and repeat the activity.

You may have noticed when doing the activity there were similarities in the last two boxes and if not, take a few minutes to have a look and see if you can see any. There may also be differences in those two boxes, and you might be wondering where they came from. There are lots of different possibilities for those things... some of which we will look at in the next section. Ultimately, everything else is what we have learnt by choice or force. By that, I mean things we have chosen to seek out and learn about or things that we have learnt from the people we have encountered in our life.

By now, you should have at least a rough idea of your current self and how you became the person you are today. You can take more time out to reflect on this if needed. If not, join me in the next section!

Two

Have you ever found yourself wondering "what am I doing here?", "what is my purpose?", "what is the meaning of life?" or even thinking or saying things like "I didn't ask to be here, I was born and then expected to get on with this and I don't want to, I don't understand it".

All of these worries and questions are part of what is called the existential angst. Meaning they are questions and things that we don't always have a concrete answer for, and this makes us feel anxious. Most people at some point in their lives find themselves with existential worries about life. Some of us will have them when we are really young, some when we are old. This worry is a normal part of human development and as we grow and change and the people around us do the same, we can find we end up having more questions about life and its purpose.

When we don't feel we have been able to find comfort for these worries this can cause increased levels of anxiety. Prolonged periods in this state of anxiousness can lead us to isolate ourselves or become distant with those around us as a means of coping. We will look into how to manage these worries in section 9. In this section, we are going to address one of the most common existential worries "what is life" by finding out what life is for you.

In my research for this chapter I came across the dictionary definition of life which states, life is:

"the animate existence or period of animate existence of an individual".

Ok, this is all well and good as a definition. But when you are trying to find understanding and meaning, this definition is very ambiguous and open to many interpretations. So firstly, let's really break this definition down…

Animate: To give something life or make it alive.

Existence: A state of being.

Period: An interval or division of time.

If we look literally at those key words and the definition as a whole, it makes sense to say that life is about being alive for a duration of time. Well, that was helpful!... Still have no idea what it is? If we look closer at what the definition is saying, in terms of human life, it is referring to "the time you are here". Nothing more and nothing less and because of this, it suggests an infinite amount of possibilities as to how you can define, use and create life.

However, because there is no "instruction manual" on what to do with this "time" that is life it can leave many of us feeling very unsettled and overwhelmed at different stages in it. As I mentioned earlier, when we are born, we look to our primary caregivers (and family) for the manual on what to do. We learn how to live through mirroring the behaviours of those around us. Now, for some people this is great. Their primary caregivers are seemingly stable, loving, supportive and caring. They are able to demonstrate behaviours that fit with a manageable way to live. For others, this is simply not the case. Primary caregivers for some are absent, abusive and neglectful. In those instances, it can be hard to learn how to manage life and coexist with others.

Then, as we get older, we learn how to live through the people we have the most contact with, in addition to our primary caregivers. These are usually nursery staff, teachers and peers, just to name a few. This cycle of influence continues as we get older, depending on the paths we choose to take. For example, if we choose to work or not, go to college/university or not etc.

There are a few other very important influencing factors to how we come to understand and manage life and those are religious beliefs and societal cultural beliefs (laws and doctrines). These two can impact your views on life at any stage. They may be introduced to you by your parents, school or by the decision to follow a certain path in life. Either way, all of the things mentioned above will influence how you see life and how you live it.

With so many different influences on our perception of life, it is no wonder that the majority of us are left confused not knowing which way to turn. You may have noticed, one thing I have not mentioned thus far is the conscious decision to do other than you have been modelled. We will take a look at this concept a little later on. For now, let us focus on understanding what life means to you now and where those meanings have come from.

In the box below (or on a separate sheet of paper) write down what life means to you and what you do day to day as a consequence of your thoughts on what life should be like. For example,

- Is it something you "just have to put up with"?

- Is it about having a family?

- Is it about career or self-development?

- Are there rules and regulations to abide by?

Then take a moment to reflect on where that definition has come from. For example:

- Is it something you learned from people around you?

- Is it influenced by your religion or government laws?

What is life for me?

What has influenced this definition?

Now that we have taken some time in the first two
sections to reflect on ourselves and our current
understanding of life, we are going to take some time to
put all of this together.

Three

Most people reading this book will have heard this saying before. If you haven't, it basically means that too many people involved in something can mess it up. The reason I chose this saying for the title of this section is because I believe this can be true for life too. So, in section one we looked at your current self and the influences involved in becoming your current self. In the second section, we looked at your understanding of life and the influences that brought you to that understanding. In this section, we are going to look at what happens when you bring all of those things together. So basically, where you are at in your life now!

Think of yourself as a colouring book in which you would use a selection of different colours to complete the picture in front of you. You pick each colour depending on what you're colouring and what you want it to look like. The different colours are a representation of the different experiences, opinions and influences that have contributed to your understanding of life and yourself in it.

Now, just like when colouring in a picture, it's easy to make mistakes or colour over the lines and our vision, in our minds, of the final piece can sometimes be different to the actual outcome. The picture, in the end, may still be beautiful but not what you were hoping for when you started out and without starting over altogether, may not ever be.

This is just like life. As I mentioned in section two, you can make a conscious decision to do other than you have been modelled. This is important in helping you feel truly comfortable in yourself and in your life. In order to feel sure and comfortable in who you are in life or what your life is going to be like, you must sit down and look at your colours (the information from section one and two). Decide which colours you want to use to create your final picture (you and your life). This is the process of making that conscious decision about who you want to be and what you want your life to be like.

The next task is going to be about really narrowing down the parts of yourself. Which parts do you want to keep?, Which parts do you like?, Which parts are helpful but not all the time?, Which parts are self-destructive?

🔅 Tip, it's important to note that even the more negative traits, habits or feelings, when looked at from a different angle may serve a positive function in your life. For example, if you are someone who tends to have very few friends or not talk to many people. This may make you feel isolated and lonely and may feel like a negative. However, it may also protect you from being hurt (positive function).

Use the space below (or a separate sheet of paper) to create a map of all of the different parts of yourself. Use the information you collected in sections one and two to help. Assess these parts of yourself by writing one negative and one positive function for each. Then make a note of the ones you want to enhance/do more of or get better at. I have provided an example to help:

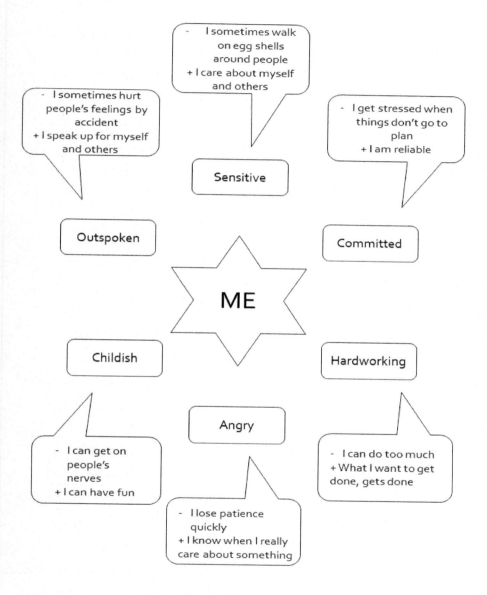

Four

"The metaphor"

Now we have done some work on understanding ourselves and our views on life, let's take a look at how to get the most out of it. In this section, I will introduce you to the metaphor that helped me, to help you get the most of it too.

***

It occurred to me, during my own journey of self-discovery, that life is a lot of hard work - as I am sure you can agree! Whilst reflecting on the struggles, tiredness and mental burnout I quite often faced, I realised that "this hard work was like having another full-time job". In fact, often it felt like having more than a full-time job, but I realised, I was right. Life was and is hard work.

The work is never-ending and can change within a second. I then began to realise that, unlike other jobs, there wasn't necessarily specific training on how to do this job of life. Well, at least I don't remember going through any formal induction process into life – Do you?. I also realised that everyone's "training" would and will be different which will produce different outcomes. It was the realisation of this (and looking at how I had used it in my life without being consciously aware of what I was doing) that led me to write this book.

As you might have guessed by now, the metaphor that I use and have been subconsciously using for years is the one of life being a job. - sounds pretty simple right? Well, just so we are on the same page, let me explain this in a bit more detail.

Let's just say you have been offered a job, any job, working anywhere. You may get to that job on your first day with some knowledge from, say previous experience in that field, of what your job requires of you. Most jobs will offer you training (in house or external) so that you are fully aware of how to do your job and what is required of you in the role. You might go to meetings during your time in your job to discuss your performance (what you are doing well or not). And in a lot of roles you will be working as part of a team or have people that you will work with or report to. Your work might directly impact others being able to do theirs and you may help people complete their tasks for the day and vice versa.

Now, let's take this and apply it to life. When we are born, we have absolutely no knowledge of this job we have been given called life. So, it's very different from applying for a job that you have previous experience in or knowledge about. This is because we have no experience of it at all! Take a second to imagine what it would be like to be given a job that you have absolutely no experience in. Some of you may have had this actually happen in your life - sounds hard right? Exactly! So when you have just been born, it would be hard for anyone to expect you to know exactly what to do in life when you have no previous experience of it. I find the reason a lot of people struggle in life is because of expectations placed on them which are outside of their experience. For example, knowing how to manage money or knowing how to cope with difficult emotions. So, where do we get this experience from?

Well, it is the responsibility of our primary caregivers/parents to provide us with the "training" so we can have the knowledge to be able to go out there and "apply" for jobs. Essentially, they aid us in our understanding of life through their behaviours, what they say and what they teach us or ask us to do. The process of growing up with the people around us gives us our initial knowledge/experience in our job called life. Then, we may go to nursery and or school and meet people such as teachers, support staff, nursery workers etc. They will also provide us with knowledge and aid our experience of how to do our job called life through the things they teach us.

This cycle continues depending on where your life takes you and the people you meet. When talking about getting a job I mentioned having managers and working as part of a team. This is also something that directly applies to the metaphor of life as a job. Our managers and team members are our parents, teachers, friends, support workers, counsellors etc. We often meet with these people and are given guidance, skills and tips. Then it becomes our choice as to whether we use these meetings to influence our "performance" in our job of life. For example, if we don't know how to do something or we are unsure of something, we can speak to people who are more experienced than us to find out what we need to know. This is a great way of you keeping yourself on track and progressing in a supported and comfortable way. Just like you would expect to be at work.

The key difference I noticed between an employed job and the job of life when writing this chapter, is that unlike an employed job there is no right way to do "life". In an employed job, your manager will inform you of what you need to do and how you need to do it which means if you deviate from this, they will tell you that you aren't doing it right. Whereas, in life, how you choose to "do it" is entirely down to you.

When you are young, there may be reasons why you can't do things the way you want and when you want to. However, this does not mean you can never do it. The beautiful thing about life is that when you put your mind to anything, you have the opportunity to have it. Perspective is always key! If you start to see life as a journey full of endless opportunities, with bumps along the way, but with the right support these bumps can be supported and sometimes prevented too.

As we saw earlier, the definition of life actually has no right or wrong connotations around it. This means when thinking about the "right" way to do life, the word "right" is subjective to you. This means that you have to decide what is the right thing for your life. This will be based on your life experiences so far (which we looked at in sections one and two) and will change as you change and grow and as the people around you do the same.

💡 Tip: Instead of telling yourself you are not doing it right or that you are doing it wrong, try telling yourself you are doing everything right for right now.

A phrase I like to say and remind myself of is "The world is your Oyster". This phrase can be used to remind us that at the right time, you will be able to do anything and go anywhere you want. This isn't always going to feel fun and at times it might feel daunting or anxiety provoking. However, if you can remind yourself of this phrase and what you have learned so far from this book you will allow your mind to be more open to choices and experiences. This, in turn, will enable you to do anything you want to do.

You may have noticed that I have skipped one vital part of the process of getting the job and that is the process of creating your CV, finding opportunities you are interested in, applying for jobs and being interviewed. These will be covered in the next sections.

For this section, we are going to look at who the biggest influences in your journey of life are right now. Who are your "managers" and "team members"? Who do you go to for support and to make sure you are on the "right track"? Using the outline of a hand on the next page, identify the 5 most influential people to your journey of life right now by writing one person in each of the fingers. These people might not be the same people as you had growing up and they may change often depending on where you go, who you meet and who inspires you.

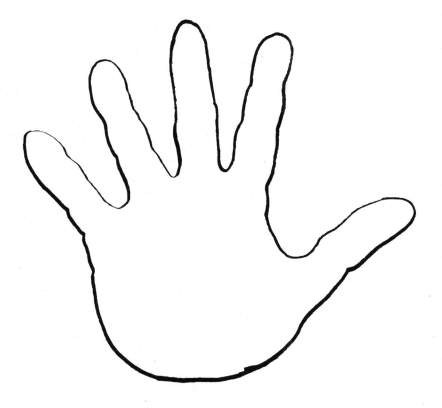

Once you have completed this task, use the space below, or a separate piece of paper to take a moment to think about how these managers and team members impact the "work" you are doing now. For example, are they people who encourage and or support you? Or are they people that do the opposite. Then ask yourself, "what are the consequences of their impact on my work?

From doing this, you may come to realise that you want or need to change some of your current managers and or team members. We will come back to this in section 8. For now, we are going to find out more about who you are.

Five

"You are what you know now and what you are yet to become"

- Self For Help

As I mentioned in the previous section, life is and can be understood in terms of a job. Now, if you have never had a job, this metaphor may not completely resonate with you but that's ok you can still go on to use this book and work through the following sections. It will help you in your life and in your considerations when you start to look for a job and apply for them.

So, before you can apply for any job you need to create a CV to inform prospective employers of your skills, achievements and abilities. This document helps employers decide if you are suitable for the position they are offering. Using the information from the sections one, two, three and four we are going to create your CV for life to help you fully understand the metaphor, how to use it and how to get the most out of your life. The sections on the following pages can be filled out here or on a separate sheet:

About you:

Name:

Date of birth:

Address:

Age:

Personal profile *(highlight specific qualities you have from sections one, two and three. Remember even the ones that you consider to be negative can have their uses so what does that tell someone about you and what you can bring to life?)*:

Experience and employment history (*list the things you have been through, experienced, achieved, responsibilities, skills and achievements*):

Education and qualifications (*in this section, list all of your education and qualifications so far, you can include certificates you have gained at school or college or events that aren't professional qualifications put a little star next to the ones you enjoyed*):

Hobbies and interests: (*List here all of the things you are interested in, these can be things you have done or tried or things you would love to try one day if you had the chance*):

When you have finished, take a look at everything you have written down for each section and take a moment to reflect on the following questions:

- What does your CV tell you about the type of person you are?
- What does your CV suggest you would be good at in life?
- Where in life would your skills and experience best be used?
- What does your CV tell you about what you like and don't like?

There is space for you to note down your answers or reflections, below:

Six

"Find what you love and DO IT - Self For Help"

Now you have your CV, let's find your dream "position". In order to apply for jobs, you will have some idea of the type of job you want to do. This will be based on where you think you are in your life, the jobs that you have seen others do, your age and what's available around you. For example, if it is your first job you might think about retail or if you have other commitments you might be looking for part-time work. In the previous sections, we looked at you, your understanding of life and what you want to keep, lose or enhance. In this section, we are going to take a look inside of you to "search" for your dream position in the job field you are working in - life. We are going to formulate the life you want!

In this section and the next, I have chosen a few key questions for you to answer that will help you identify and cultivate your dream position. They will also help you reflect on if you have everything you need to live the life you want. You might want to get some paper or a notebook to note down any questions and or thoughts that come up whilst doing this section.

Ok, so let's jump straight in. The first question and probably the hardest of all the questions is "what do you want your life to be like?" By this I mean, what do you want from your life, what do you want to do and achieve. The reason I mentioned that this was one of the hardest questions is because it is often hard for people to imagine what they want for their lives. This is because these thoughts are often followed with a trail of negative thoughts that convince you of a number of reasons why you can't have what you want to in life.

Now, before you answer this question, I want you to take a moment to consider the question in a different way. Imagine for just a moment, that you have everything your heart desired. Imagine that money, time and experience are not in the way and that you have an infinite amount of money, time and experience. Imagine you are doing whatever your heart desires without negative thoughts creeping in, telling you that you are not good enough. Imagine you had no one telling you what you wanted was not achievable or that it was a bad idea. Imagine you had no one in your life telling you they "wanted you to do something different because it is more sensible". Imagine there was absolutely nothing stopping you from getting what you want…

Now, I will ask you again, what do you want your life to be like? In the space below or on a separate piece of paper, create a wish list for your life (your goals). This can be in words or pictures, whatever works best for you. Remember, when doing this activity, I want you to think with no limits. If money, time, location or anything like that was not something you needed to consider, what would your life look like? *(I have added some key areas of life for you to think about to help with this, you can also add your own)*

Relationships, Family, Health, Career/business, Mental health, Finance, Social life:

And there you have it, your dream position as of right now! I say as of right now as this will often change at different points in your life and that is ok... if you need to do this exercise again at another point in your life because things have changed... go for it!

Seven

"The interview"

In section five we created your CV and in section six we found your dream position. In this section, we are going to interview you for the position (the life that you want to live). To do this, take a look back at your CV and your dream position and ask yourself the following question:

"Do I currently have all of the skills, qualities, experience and knowledge to get to the goals I want to achieve?"

If you do, then great!... If not, ask yourself...

"What might I need to get to that goal?"

Now, this second interview question should be a lot easier than the first one. This is because it's often the case that we are more able to point out the negatives/what we don't have, than the positives/what we do have.

There may be some goals that you are not sure what qualities, skills, knowledge and experience you will need. This is OK. If this is the case, do some research, it might be that you want to become a director of a TV company for example, but you are not sure how you can do that. Take a look at the job role online and research the type of experience you need to have to get into that position.

It might be that you want to improve your mental health, but you don't know how. That is also ok. Find people who have managed to improve their mental health or seek professional support from a therapist or your doctor. Use people who do have the knowledge can help you identify the steps you need to take to meet that goal.

For some of your goals, it may not be the case that you need to do practical research. For example, you may have a goal around friendships or bringing more positivity into your life. In which case you might want to consider going to social occasions or assessing the friendships you have. You may also want to consider letting go of friendships that don't bring positivity into your life.

Take a moment to write down what you would need to do/change to get to your end goal (your dream position). There are lots of different things you can try/do to get to each goal you want to achieve. Sometimes this can feel really overwhelming or confusing. I have provided two diagrams on the next pages to help with this:

Bridge: Imagine you are standing at the start of the bridge on the grass. And when you get to the other side you have successfully completed your goal. What steps would you need to take to get to the other side?

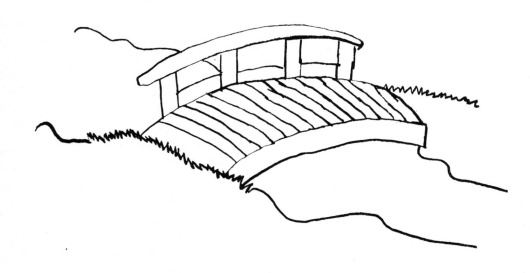

Spider web: When there are multiple ways you can get to the end goal, try imagining you are standing in the middle of a spider web. Each line outwards represents a possible path you could take to get to your end goal... What would be the possible paths you could take and what steps would you need to take in each path?

There are some blank pages next, for you to write out the steps for each of your goals either in your own way or using the two diagrams provided.

Eight

"The first day of the rest of your life"

Congratulations! You have been accepted for the role and the start date is today! Now, let's have a look at your managers and team members to make sure you can do everything that you need to do, to get your job done successfully...

It's important when making any change in life to consider the influences around you. So, for example, if you need to learn about business, who do you know that knows about running a business that could support you through that process. This person would be a mentor (or as per our analogy, your "manager or team member"), someone who has been through or done what you want to. Someone who can help guide you in your journey to where you want to be.

These people could also be lecturers, friends, family... literally, anyone - the choice is yours. There may be someone that you would love to be your mentor however, you don't know them or can't afford to access them... That is ok, in these instances, this is where the internet will become your best friend! You can find people online who have been mentored by the person who would be your ideal mentor or even videos or information from your ideal mentor. You can have as many of these people in your life that you like, and you may already have some. As we did in section four, use the hand on the next page to identify 5 people (one in each finger) as your teammates/mentors/managers that can help you with your new position. These might be the same as the people you identified in section four, but they might be different depending on your goals and vision. They also may be people who can help you stay on track, like an accountability buddy. Someone who can check in on you and remind you of the things you said you would like to do.

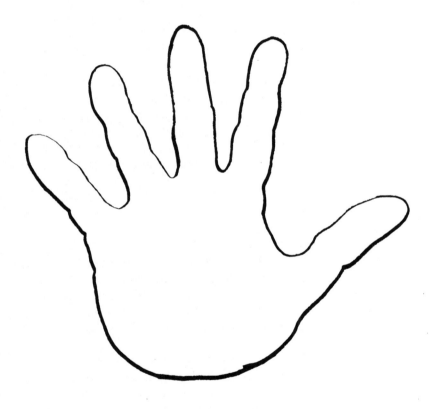

Nine

"The ability to self soothe is one of the most important gifts of life" - Self For Help

Now, there may be some who have got to this section and realised there are still things that are unknown. Or, as I mentioned in section 2, some who know what they want and what they need to do but are faced with anxiety around this. In this section, we are going to look at how to manage the anxiety of not knowing but also anxiety in general, as I'm aware the process of going through the sections of this book may have brought up feelings of anxiety for some people... So, let's get straight in!

- **Be kind to yourself** - This has to be one of the most important things you can do. If you have ever been bullied, then you will know it is hard to be happy when "someone" is being mean to you every day, don't let that someone be you!

  💡 Create a list of positive affirmations or statements you can say to yourself. Say these to yourself during times when you know you are feeling low or emotionally rocky. Use these to help bring you out of that place and back on track.

- **Communicate** – This is usually the hardest thing for people to do. However, the more you do it, the easier it gets. As we looked at in the previous section, you can talk to people who have been through what you are going through. This isn't just useful for guidance on how to get support. It is also useful to hear knowledge on the magnitude of ways there are to cope. Knowledge on how to get through things and provides opportunities to test out things that might work for you too.

- ## Get professional help - This ties in with the point above. Professionals in helping people manage their life or manage their emotions are people who have both personal and professional experience. They want to share this with you, so take them up on it to help you get to where you want to be and maybe one day you could become someone who shares too.

- ## Reassure yourself - This I mean very literally, tell yourself "you are going to be ok" tell yourself "it is going to be ok". Have you ever felt anxious and a deep desire to have your person of choice give you a hug or say something to you that you know "makes you feel better"? Well, that person can also be you. The people that comfort us are not always available to do so. This is why it is important to be able to do it for ourselves. This process is called self-soothing.

💡 Make a list of the things people around you do to make you feel better when you are sad or anxious. Then when you are faced with situations that make you feel these ways, take a look at the list and do or say one of those things for yourself.

- **Distract yourself** - Keep a list of your goals nearby with the reasons you want to achieve them. During times of anxiousness, look back at this list to distract yourself from the feelings of anxiety. Focus your mind on the reasons why you want to achieve your goals.

- **Acknowledge your anxiety** - Your anxiety is there for a reason and it's because it's trying to protect you from something. There is a fear in you that you are unable to cope and it's important to acknowledge its existence. Ask yourself, is this anxiety helping me or stopping me from achieving my goals? If it's stopping you, then ask it to go away for the moment. Tell it, it is not needed right now but it will have its use in a different situation when you need to be afraid to protect yourself from harm.

Conclusion

And there you have it! I would like to thank you for purchasing this book and taking the time out for yourself to make a difference in your life.

Having reached the end you should have a better understanding of the following:

- ❖ Who you are and why.
- ❖ What life means to you.
- ❖ Where you are in your life.
- ❖ Where you want to be in your life.
- ❖ How you can get to where you want to be.
- ❖ What support you have/need.
- ❖ How to deal with the fear that comes with making a change.

Remember, the world is your oyster. Now you have all of this knowledge, what will you do with it?

***

Good luck!

Printed in Great Britain
by Amazon

23299511R00030